BREATHE

BREATHE

PEARLIE M. WALKER

Warrior Princess Nation, LLC

Copyright © 2021 by Pearlie M. Walker

All rights reserved. No part of this book may be reproduced in any manner whatsoever without the written permission of the publisher except in the case of brief quotations embodied in critical articles and reviews.

Published by Warrior Princess Nation, LLC
North Las Vegas, NV
For information email admin@warriorprincessnation.com

First Printing, 2021

Unless otherwise noted all Scriptures are taken from the KJV. Scriptures marked KJV are taken from the KING JAMES VERSION (KJV): KING JAMES VERSION, public domain.

Italics added to Scripture quotations are the author's own emphasis.

Contents

Introduction — 1

Forward — 3

One
City Life — 9

Two
First Love — 17

Three
Caught Up Again — 22

Four
Unfit to the Core — 25

Five
Crushed — 28

Six
Prison Life — 33

Seven
I's Married Now — 38

Eight
Fear or Fear Not — 40

Nine
Mending the Past — 43

Ten
Back in Chicago — 46

Eleven
Saved Now — 52

Twelve
Inhale and Exhale — 55

Thirteen
Voice of God — 58

Fourteen
Eyes on Jesus — 61

Fifteen
Life in Christ — 64

Sixteen
The Power of Real Love — 67

Seventeen
Affirmation — 70

About The Author — 73

Dedication

I want to give honor and glory to my Lord and Savior Christ Jesus. He is truly the one who inspired me to write this book.
I dedicate this book to my loving husband, Melvin, six children, fifteen grandchildren, and eight great-grandchildren. They have given me the strength to pursue writing.
I always knew that there was a story to be told, even though I wasn't sure how or when I would tell my story. So many years have prepared me for what I am about to share.

Introduction

For years I've received prophecies regarding writing books. I remember one prominent Prophet, Shawn Boltz, who came to our city. He spoke at The Mission, one of our local churches in the Vacaville, CA area. In his prophecy, he confirmed the writing of books. He said that I was like a Moses; I was called to deliver the people. However, I still did not move on it right away because here it is, now three years later, and I am just now writing the first book.

I believe this is the time God is breathing His breath on me to write this book. We are living in unprecedented times. I look around and see so many people hurting, suffering, and dying. So much devastation all around us. The world we live in is not like I once knew it to be. Uncertainty is everywhere. You can see the fear in people's eyes, and hope becomes hopeless. We need intervention from Christ Jesus, and I feel now is the time for me to speak out and encourage people that there is still hope. No matter what we are faced with or going through, there is still hope. We must hold our heads up and look to the one who is in control of all things. My heart is so heavy for our world and the people in it.

I can understand things far better now than I could when I first heard those words, 'write the book.' So it is now time for me to tell my story and help others know they can make it even in a world full of uncertainty.

I remember a saying from the movie Forrest Gump[1], "Life is like a box of chocolates. You never know what you're going to get." It is so true. You never know what life is going to throw you. From the time you were conceived until life ends, your journey is a process. So, let's take a moment and breathe.

[1] Roth, Eric, Forest Gump (The movie), 1994, The Tisch Company

Forward

Spiritual Realm

We must understand that our very existence comes from a higher existence. The word of God says in Genesis 1:27, "So God created man in his own image, in the image of God created he him; male and female created he them." This Scripture lets us see that we were created in the image of our God and in him exist both male and female. He created us in such a way that we could see him in each of us. This is why Jesus could say to Philip he had been with him so long, and yet he did not see God, the Father. (John 14:8-9) After creating man, God even went further to cause man to become a living soul.

Genesis 2:7 reads, "And the Lord God formed man of the dust of the ground and breathed into his nostrils the breath of life, and man became a living soul." In this passage of Scripture, we must see that God blew himself, His Spirit, into the very nostrils of man so that he would become a living soul. The very Creator of creation was kind enough to breathe into us his life. That which is holy and perfect. Hallelujah!! Glory to the Most High for His infinite love for us.

God loved us so much that He gave us all of Himself. This was done so that man would have all of God's given authority and creativity. In the beginning, His plans were for us to be in total fellowship with Him. To become high priest ministers of God. He never intended for man to suffer hurt, pain, or die. His plans were perfect for us. He created a garden of paradise for us to live in and provided everything in that garden that we needed.

God's love is so perfect that we've overlooked the essence of the beauty that it brings. The breath of life He has given us is so precious, and yet we don't take time out to inhale and exhale His breath, Spirit, to smell the fragrance of His love. It is essential as humans to acknowledge the Creator of all creation. To know that His intent for us is to allow us to understand how to relax in Him and rest. Some Scriptures come to mind concerning resting in the Lord.

> *Thus saith the Lord God unto these bones; Behold, I will cause breath to enter you, and ye shall live.* **Ezekiel 37:5**

> *Casting all your care upon him; for he cares for you.* **1 Peter 5:7**

Truly my soul waited upon God: from him cometh my salvation. **Psalm 62:1**

Behold the fowls of the air: for they sow not, neither do they reap, nor gather into barns; yet your heavenly Father feedeth them. Are ye not much better than they? **Matthew 6:26**

Rejoice in the Lord always: and again, I say, Rejoice. Let your moderation be known unto all men. The Lord is at hand. Be careful of nothing; but in everything by prayer and supplication with thanksgiving let your requests be made known unto God. And the peace of God, which passeth all understanding, shall keep your hearts and minds through Christ Jesus. **Philippians 4:4-7**

The Lord will give strength unto his people, the Lord will bless his people with peace. **Psalm 29:11**

Come unto me, all ye that labour and are heavy laden, and I will give you rest. Take my yoke upon you and learn of me; for I am meek and lowly in heart: and ye shall find rest unto your souls. For my yoke is easy, and my burden is light. **Matthew 11:28-30**

These things I have spoken unto you, that in me ye might have peace. In the world ye shall have tribulation: but be of good cheer; I have overcome the world. **John 16:33**

Let everything that hath breath praise the Lord, Praise ye the Lord. **Psalm 150:6**

And he said, my presence shall go with thee, and I will give thee rest. **Exodus 33:14**

In life, we have many trials and tribulations which can overwhelm us. One thing for sure, as long as we have the breath of life on the inside of us, we can make it through any trial or tribulation. I am writing this book to encourage you and help you understand that you cannot and will not be defeated as long as you have God on your side. Not in any of life's circumstances, trials or tribulations. We must learn how to breathe. We must remember to inhale and exhale. Breathe in and breathe out. Breathing is most essential to our living. Without breath, we cannot live at all.

Sabbath Day

Rest is vital to your spiritual walk with the Lord. Unfortunately, many Christians today don't appreciate the value of rest or keeping the Sabbath day holy. Rest will allow our mind, body, and soul to renew and restart with more strength and focus. As we rest in the word of God, it also allows us to have hope in the trials and tribulations we encounter throughout our lifetime. With the proper understanding that God's word is active and powerful, it will bring rest to our minds and increase our faith to know we have the victory.

Fall of Man

I remember my Apostle, Tyrone Holland, use to say, "in every good seed sowing service, the old adversary is always lurking around to steal it." This is what Satan accomplished when he approached Eve in the garden.

Now the serpent was more subtil than any beast of the field which the LORD God had made. And he said unto the woman, Yea, hath God said, Ye shall not eat of every tree of the garden? And the woman said unto the serpent, We may eat of the fruit of the trees of the garden: but of the fruit of the tree which *is* in the midst of the garden, God hath said, Ye shall not eat of it, neither shall ye touch it, lest ye die. And the serpent said unto the woman, Ye shall not surely die: Genesis 3:1-4

These Scriptures let us see clearly the beginning of deception and the fall of man. The enemy had defeated Eve by causing her and Adam to doubt God's word and set the course for the fall of man. Doubt brings about disobedience which opens the door to all of mankind's suffering, sickness, disease, and unbelieve.

A perfect plan of God was tainted by the lies of Satan. His plan was to destroy the image of God as well as His word. Since his deception, we now experience the opposite of what was really meant for our lives. But our lives became in such disarray when Satan intervene in the plans of our God (Elohim).

This is why I know it is important to share my story about God's plan of salvation for my life. So that we can all understand the God (Elohim), we serve and why He created us to worship Him with our very lives.

I heard Holy Spirit speak to me and saying that I was born for such a time as this. Therefore, it is time to share my life story for the masses to see how He has breathed on mankind in every area of their lives.

One

City Life

I remember growing up in the housing projects in the inner city of St. Louis, Missouri. I was around five years old when my parents moved there. Growing up in this environment can bring on many fears because there was never a dull moment. You witnessed killings, division between the families, kids bullying you in the neighborhood or school, and sometimes there was hardly enough food to feed your family.

My father was a hardworking man who worked for the Pacific Railroads. He was tall, handsome, and a very meek man. My brothers and I don't have a lot of childhood memories of him. My mother was very young when they got married. My father was sixty-five, and she was twenty-five. In those days, her occupation was a stay-at-home mom.

Even though my father worked hard, we sometimes would only have just enough to get by. As a result, there would be times I would hear my parents debating between feeding us kids or paying certain bills. I would always hear my father tell my mom not to worry that God would come through for us. I can remember one time before he could get those words out of his mouth, a neighbor stopped by; he had been fishing and wanted to share some of his catch with my parents.

My father would refuse the neighbor sometimes out of pride. But, then, he would go out and come back himself with food for us. I remember thinking as a child that God would always provide. At that moment and time, God was breathing on our family situation. I believe the words that my father had spoken in faith activated the hand of God to move on our behalf.

As a young girl, I don't remember my mother or father attending church. I do know that my father believed in the Catholic religion. My mother never talked about God to my knowledge. Both of my parents were worldly people. My father drank a lot when we were growing up. I can remember him being outside with other neighbors sitting and drinking wine. My mother would call down to him to come in the house. Eventually, she started to have her own agenda.

The neighbor that stopped by to bring fish one day would

> **Breathe:** I hear Holy Spirit speaking right now. Someone's faith isn't where it should be at this moment. He wants me to tell you that everything is going to be alright. That He has heard your prayers about certain things, and He is answering you right now. I don't know who needed to hear that word. Oh! But! God! He is also saying rest in him let your confidence be built upon a solid rock, His son, Christ Jesus. Sometimes you have to go through something to even appreciate what God is doing in your life or what He has done in your life. Either way, He is breathing on you right now. Take a moment and inhale and exhale.

become my worse nightmare. My mother started a relationship with this neighbor, which lasted for many years. Occasionally, she would send me to meet this person in our building's stairway to get money or gifts that he would buy her. Little did she know she was setting me up as a temptation for her boyfriend. I will not get into all the details, but he started foundling my private areas after a few of those trips.

At first, he would say it was okay, and no one needed to know about it. This type of behavior continued for a long time. I begin to ask myself what I did to deserve this. Why? Why would he want to do this to me? I sometimes cried and begged my mother not to send me, hoping it would give her some clue of what was happening. No, not one time did she acknowledge my behavior. Sometimes, I felt like she knew what this man was doing to me and just didn't care about me, only thinking of herself. As my mother became more involved with her new man, she decided to leave my father.

One day after my father went to work, she packed my brothers and me up and moved out into her own place. I cried, confused about why she was leaving our father. As a young girl, all I could see was a hardworking man who was providing for his family; oh, how I loved my father. I didn't know anything about his demons, except for the fact that he did drink a lot.

During this time in my life, I became a very angry and rebellious young girl. I loved my father very much, and I was angry with my mother for leaving him. I did not understand why adults did what they did, so I became defiant toward my mother. I began to run away from home and play hooky from school.

A year later, my father passed away; I was only ten years old. This devastated me, and I grew even angrier. I started experimenting with drugs and alcohol. As young as I was, I even began to experiment with sex. I was hurting inside and needed love, and I was looking for it in all the wrong places. I had been brainwashed not to tell anyone about this sexual abuse, and now with my father gone, I felt trapped inside. His passing was so painful for me it felt my whole life had just stopped. Two more years went by at the hands of this sexual predator; it felt like a lifetime of agony and pain.

By the time I was twelve years old, I was out of control, and my mother couldn't do anything with me. Several times I was taken away from her and sent to live with other people. School authorities would even take me in because they believed in me, but I didn't want to hear that. In my eyes, adults were just a bunch of liars and mixed-up people.

I fell in the hands of some of my own family members who were drug dealers and users; I became a product of the streets and the world. Whatever it had in it, I tasted it. There was no limit to the things I did in the world. I never told anyone all those years, the trap was set, and I was the prey. I started dressing older so that I could attract older men. I learned that we could get things from men and money, so I started using sex as a weapon. I began to use my molestation to my advantage. I held it over that man's head and begin to desire those things my mother was getting.

I am not proud; I am just transparent. I know that I am not the only one who has experienced molestation; it, unfortunately, happens all the time.

Life went on, and let me tell you, I did not stop with the things I was doing. I was caught up in the snares of life. I did not know how to break free from this pit I was in. I was bound in all things and hopeless. The adversary had me entangled in the snares of this world but let me tell you, I thought I was having the time of my life.

> **Breathe**: It is liberating to be able to share things that have happened to us in life. It gives us an opportunity to thank the Lord for bringing us out of those situations. Don't keep it to yourself; tell someone what is happening or has happened to you. That old saying what happens in this house stays in this house, was a lie to keep you in bondage.

> **Breathe**: I hear Holy Spirit speaking. He is bringing you out of that situation. He is breathing on it right now. He says vengeance belongs to Him, and He will avenge your enemy for what he has done to you. Know that your reward is great in the earth and in heaven for all that you have gone through. Nothing escapes His eyes. He is always watching over you in the good and bad.

For the eyes of the Lord run to and fro throughout the whole earth, to shew himself strong on the behalf of them whose heart is perfect toward Him. **II Chronicles 16:9**

Even though my siblings and I were growing up in the urban life of the inner city, it was one of the worse times in my life. The bitterness, anger, and resentment had caused me to hate life. I hated everyone and everything. There were times I just didn't want to live anymore. The alcohol and drug use made me feel numb from the hurt and pain I was feeling inside. Yet my heavenly Father kept His eyes on me as well as the abuser. So I forgave him as the years went on.

As children, we don't understand certain things, but I realized we have no control over some things as I grew older. It's shocking and hurts when these things happen to you or a loved one. Families suffer when this type of spirit is in operation. There seemed to be no one in my life to protect me and keep me out of harm's way. Then, many years later, my mother came to live with me in California, and I could also forgive my mother. I had come to understand by then that forgiveness was for me, not the other person. It takes power away from the other person.

Remember all these things happened when man fell from the grace of God. It was never His intent for you or me to suffer at the hands of an abuser. I promise you will be able to forgive and live a normal life again, one that you feel worthy of living.

Breathe: I pray right now that the years stolen from your life will be restored with love, joy, peace, grace, and mercy. That the Lord blesses you with every good and perfect gift from above. Let the Lord restore you from anything the cankerworms, caterpillar, and the palmerworm have eaten out of your life. (Joel 2:25) Know that your God is bigger than the molestation or whatever happened to you. He does love you.

Breathe: Take a moment to look at the person in the mirror, you, and tell yourself how much you appreciate you for being there with you through it all. Know that you will live your best life ever.

Breathe: Again, breathe and give yourself permission to let it all go. This is what the Sovereign Lord says: Look! I am going to put breath into you and make you live again! (Ezekiel 37:5). He knows about the pain, the hurt, and the anger you are feeling right now. He died so that you may be set free from the bondage of those spirits. Let Him complete His work in your life. This too shall pass, and you will be alright. God has to help you overcome it because its burden is too much for you to carry.

Two

First Love

Even though my mother left my father, they never divorced. So, when he passed away, she was the beneficiary of his life insurance policy. So she went and bought herself a home in the St. Louis County area. No more city life; we were moving on up. I'm sure she hoped that this would make a difference in her children's lives. So we started a new life, new schools, and making new friends. When we moved into our new home, I was an eighth-grader, last year of middle school.

After about six months of settling into our new community, schools, and meeting new people, I met a high school student I started dating. He was a wrestler on the Maplewood High School varsity team. I used to love going to his wrestling matches; he was good at it. He was good-looking, kind, someone, a girl, dreamed of marrying. We fell in love with each other; during this time, he was seventeen, and I was only fifteen. Love! What did we know about that? Anyway, we thought we did. Before graduating from middle school, I got pregnant, and we had our first child. She was a beautiful baby girl, and we were so in love with her.

We were going to have this wonderful fairytale romance, the house with the white picket fence around it and a life that would be filled with love forever. At least that's what I thought. Then, two years later, he graduated from high school, his mother encouraged him to go into the U.S. Army. He followed the advice of his mother, joined the military, and was stationed in Korea.

There I was, all alone to raise our now two-year-old daughter by myself. Again, trapped, the dreams of a fairytale romance and the house with the white picket fence are gone. Shortly after he left, I immediately turned back to my old ways, the worldly life of the streets. My old lifestyle of drugs, sex, and alcohol. Even though I had a child, it did not matter; I didn't care about life. To me, anyone who loved me always left. I asked my mother one weekend could one of my brothers babysit for me, and I did not return for several days. My mother became very frustrated with me and my destructive lifestyle. I was hurting everyone I was around, and she put her foot down. My brothers could no longer babysit, and I was no longer allowed in her home. Ugh! Don't judge me.

A year later, my first love returned home from his tour in Korea. When he got home, he found me caught up in a life of destruction and sin that was unstoppable. Even though he was home, I continued to do those things I was doing. I was in an adulterous, fornication lifestyle now, sleeping around like some common slut that just needed a man. He chose to still stay with me and put up with this lifestyle of mine. He was military; there wasn't much he could do about it anyway. He was under military authority. He would have to leave anytime they sent orders to go to the next place. He was stationed closer to home this time, so he asked our daughter and me to join him. I knew he loved me but, and in his mind, I know he was hoping this would help me come out of this life of destruction and sin.

We married, and I was so elated that we could be together and raise our daughter. But the demons inside of me would not let me be that mother or wife. Although he had come to get us, I still was living the same type of evil lifestyle. We spent two years living on the military base while he finished out his stay in the army. In those two years, life would become a nightmare for us. I was cheating on him with every available John. Finally, he got to the point where he couldn't take my out-of-control behavior anymore. We argued and fought a lot, but I didn't care. I was going to do what I wanted to do; he could love me or leave me. I was wild and out of control even in our marriage. After he completed his stay, we relocated back to our hometown, where he found a job as a mechanic. He loved working on cars, and that became his trade. Somewhere between the fighting and my adulteries, we went on to have three more children together.

His family started to interfere in our relationship, especially his mother and older sisters. His family didn't care for me and felt I wasn't good enough for him. I wasn't the type of girl they saw him with. His mother was overprotective of him even after we married and have a family. All she wanted was for her son to take care of her and entailed giving her all his money. So, his mother, out of her frustration with our relationship, began telling him that certain children were not his and began to plant doubt in his mind. These accusations caused a division between his family and us for many years. When it was all said and done, we split up. We were never divorced, just went our separate ways. I walked off, leaving him and my children once again for my old lifestyle of the streets.

Our relationship would never have the peace and blessing from our families because of my lifestyle. I take complete responsibility for what happened to this family. Many, many years of hurt, pain, and still to this day, unforgiveness. I pray one day that they forgive me, and we can at least come together.

> **Breathe**: Right now, I am interceding for the families that the enemy is and has attacked, causing division within them. I pray that they come together in prayer and fasting for one another. I ask you, Heavenly Father, to heal every person affected by their parent's choices. Heavenly Father, forgive me right now for all of the hurt and pain I caused. I realize and understand now that I could only give what I had inside of me. I was breathing out the pain and hurt inside of me onto my husband and children.

My children didn't deserve that; my selfish lifestyle caused them to not have a typical home with both mother and father. A mother who didn't care about anything except her own life of the streets and what was in them. It is sad to say the streets have a language and lifestyle that can leave you hooked for years. It was my choices that led to this family never being able to know true love and peace. They deserved more, and I didn't have it in me to give them. Their father tried to put it back together to be a family, but I was just out of control to the point of no return. I needed intervention, and no one in my life could intervene to help me turn it around.

Three

Caught Up Again

As life goes on you, do what you have to do. But, unfortunately, here is where things get more complicated than they already are in my life. December 25, 1975, five days before Christmas, I found myself looking through jail bars because I had taken my evil to another level. It was a dreary evening; while everyone was busy doing last-minute shopping, I was one of those who were out doing their last-minute crime. What a mistake this was. I should have stayed at home.

An acquaintance of my mine told me about this place you could pass off some checks. So off I go to this check cashing place trying to cash a bogus check to support my drug and alcohol addictions. After giving the clerk the check, I stand there like a dummy, thinking the teller would give me the money when in walks the police authority.

The clerk told them I was trying to pass on a check that he verified was not mine. I'm trying to talk my way out of this situation when the police told me he was taking me to the St. Louis city jail. I was astounded at the words coming out of his mouth. I know I shouldn't have been, so I just began to break down and cry. The officer handcuffed me, placed me in the back of the patrol car, and arranged to have my car towed away. Here I was off to jail for the holidays instead of going home. I cried even harder, knowing that my choices had caused more chaos in my life once again.

> *Cast all your anxiety on him because he cares for you.* ***1 Peter 5:7***

Breathe: Holy Spirit is speaking to those who know the feeling or are currently locked up. He is with you always to the ends of the earth. He will never leave you or forsake you even in times like this.

Four

Unfit to the Core

I left my children at home alone. They were tiny, the oldest was going on seven years old, and my youngest was just a baby. I know what you're thinking honey, what kind of mother is this. You're right to ask that question; I was unfit to the core. I was locked up in a jail cell, unable to make any phone calls for a while because they had to process me. I was about to lose my mind because of how I left the home situation. I found out later that my oldest daughter opened the door for a neighbor friend who occasionally stopped by to visit. She got in touch with their father, and he came to stay with them in my apartment. With my lifestyle of drug addiction, she knew they were left alone with the possibility of me not returning anytime soon. I am so grateful for God, who made a way of escape for my little children.

I had once again chosen the wrong way of doing things. I am so glad today that I didn't take them with me on that day because the outcome would have been much different. The fears I had of them being taken and put in Child Protective Custody did happen after my stay in jail. My mother was not willing to take them. She was a single mom who had her own family to raise. I brought this on myself being rebellious. She felt that these were consequences of my own choices. So, my husband's family stepped in and took them into their homes.

Breathe: I repent for leaving my little children alone and ask for their forgiveness. I thank my Lord and Savior for the neighbor who decided to stop by for a visit. God is so good to us even in our sin. He will make a way for us out of our wilderness. To my four children, I hope and pray one day you find it in your hearts to forgive me for not being there for you the way a mother should have been. There was no excuse for my behavior. Trust and believe I do love each and every one of you. I see clearly now that the Lord has breathed on me and has changed my whole life.

Five

Crushed

This time I am trapped and can't get my way out. Finally, after about two days in jail, I could make a phone call to someone. I called my mother, and until this day of deliverance, I regretted ever making that call. She swore at me and told me how she felt about me being in jail. She went as far as to say for me not to call back because there was nothing she would do to help me.

It felt like she had taken a dagger, placed it in my heart, and turned it over and over again. Yes, I understand I did this to myself, but it was my mother's words that now rang in my spirit. As I went back into that cell and laid down on that cold hard steel. I cried and cried until I just couldn't cry anymore; I was CRUSHED.

I was crushed by her words. I tried for many years to get her words out of my mind. But, they just wouldn't go away; they stayed, they torment me. You see, torment is a spirit, and it stayed around for a lot of years. Those words crushed me until I felt I could not be put back together again. Most of my family had turned their backs on me. Why not? I was the rotten apple in the bunch. In those days, you were called the black sheep of the family. I had done so much evil that everyone I knew had washed their hands of me. I can say rightfully so today. Remember, I am holding myself accountable for this life I lived.

While still in the city jail, I heard a voice from the cell next to me asking if I smoked, and I said, "yes." The person reached around to my cell and handed me a Lucky Strike cigarette. I thanked him and began to puff on that cigarette which calmed me for a moment. Crushed! Crushed by everything happening around me. Here I was, a wretch undone, nothing going right in my life. Even when I think I am trying to make it right, it was going wrong. Crushed! Can't get my way out of this.

Over and over in my head were all the questions. What's going to happen now? How much time will I get for the charges they have on me? My children are out there; what is happening to my babies right now? Are they okay? Who cares about me, poor me? Why did I do this to myself? Oh, Lord, help me, I can't do this. I am about to lose my mind. Locked

> **Breathe:** I am praying for every person right now that ever felt like they were unworthy because of the choices they made in their life. I pray right now that you give yourself permission to forgive yourself. I'm praying you are able to forgive any person who may have hurt you. It was many years after this happened before I could sit down with my mother and tell her I forgive her and ask her to forgive me. I am still praying for the opportunity to do the same with my four older children that I hurt. You see, the hurt that was in me from childhood until this time in my life was a vicious cycle of hurt and pain in their lives.

up, feeling hopeless about my situation, not knowing what's ahead of me.

On the second day, the guard comes and tells me that instead of going to regular court to hear the charges against me, I would be transported over to the workhouse, prison. I asked him, why? He responded by saying it was the holidays and that all judges were on vacation until the first of the year. He told me they only had one other person and me in the regular jail, so they transported us over to the city workhouse.

Crushed! I had never been in prison or jail before. I am scared out of my mind. Lord, what is going to happen to me? Please, Jesus, help me and be with me. Never called on the Lord before. Here I am now calling on the name of the Lord Jesus. I have come to realize your sins will catch up to you. Just like committing a crime, you will have to pay for whatever you do.

Here I am, face to face with all of my demons with nowhere to run or hide. Pain, hurt, lust, adultery, fornications, drug addiction, alcoholism, unfit mother, hatred for myself, they all were locked up inside of me in that prison cell. I needed deliverance, and yet it still would be more years before it would come. Lord have mercy on my soul.

I'm sitting here writing this, being set free from all the weight of guilt and shame that I've held onto for more than half my life. Set free from all the bondage associated with my sins. This, of course, was already predestined for my life. It was written into the fiber of my being. I could not stop it if I wanted to. But, God had a plan for every single thing that happens to me in this life. Even when I didn't know or understand, it had its purpose. God will always reveal His plan to us in our lives when He has our attention.

Breathe: I hear Holy Spirit saying to me someone is thinking right now. Wow! Why would you write such a book? All the things that have taken place and what you have done to hurt so many. He's telling me to answer you by saying that there is someone else in this world who is going through hurt and pain. They need to hear my story and know that it is okay to tell their story. It will also bring healing to them in their life. What we go through is always for somebody else.

Six

Prison Life

Let me pause a moment and let you know that everything I have written about up until now has set the stage for some of the most crushing blows I had ever received from family. I felt like a failure, devastated by the situation I put myself in. I want you, my reader, to understand I am taking responsibility for messing up my life and the lives of those attached to me. I am crushed to the bone a week into being a resident at the city workhouse prison. Still, no family member showed up for a visit or a phone call to inquire about my wellbeing. My mother held true to her words.

Settled down best I could for where I was. All alone to deal with strangers. It was hard for me to do so because here I was in a situation that terrified me to death. No one there for me to count on or turn to for help. No family cared enough about me to come to visit. If you have ever been locked up before, it is a place that will crush your spirit to pieces. It causes pain and agony in your heart you just can't explain. It brings forth a reality check that causes you to examine your life through and through.

One Saturday afternoon, while in the workhouse prison, we had contact visiting out in the gymnasium. Your friends and family could come in, and you were able to talk and touch each other. There I was excited. I don't know what for, there was no one coming to see me. I guess it was just the fact that I was not going to be locked behind those bars for a few hours. It made me feel some sense of freedom out in that large open area. I walked around in amazement at all the men and women who were locked up in this place. Oh! By the way, this was a co-ed prison.

As I walked around in a daze, this man walked up to me and asked my name. I shyly drew back as I was contemplating telling him my name. I really wanted to run, but there was nowhere to go. He went on to say to me, "you never been to jail before, huh?" Scared as I was, I looked at him, and I answered him back, "no." He said, "I know I can tell you're scared to death." Then he went on to introduce himself. He was right, I was looking around that room, and for the first time in my life, I believe the reality of life had set in. Here I was locked up with every walk of life that was on the streets. Yet when I

> **Breathe**: I pray right now that you be strong and that the Lord Jesus save you while you are in that jail or prison cell. That your heart turns from all that is evil and from all of your evil ways. I pray that you are delivered from the evil spirits that control your life. God is still with you even in that prison/jail cell. Turn to Him and ask Him to come into your heart and deliver you right now. He loves you just as you are and where you are. John 3:16 says, *"For God so loved the world, that he gave his only begotten Son, that whoever believeth in him should not perish, but have everlasting life."* Trust and believe God's heart is for you.

was out there in the streets, it did not bother me how it affected me right then. Boom, reality check, and God had sent the bomb. Checkmate!

I started to walk away to find a restroom and a place to sit down. When the man said to me, "don't go," I froze in my tracks. I felt like I was about to pee my pants. I turned to him and said, "I really need to go to the bathroom." He looked at me and said, "Alright, let me walk with you." I agreed, and he began to ask me questions about my situation and about me. I did not want to tell him but, somehow, I started talking, and then he complimented me on how beautiful he thought my name was. As we continued to talk, he said, "You have no one to look after you, do you?" I was shocked to see it was so obvious to him. I answered, "No!" This man stated, "I will take care of you as long as you are here, don't worry." Wow! A savior! He was going to take care of me. He would provide for me while

I was in prison. I saw myself as someone hopeless in life, never realizing at that time, I was just lost and needed a real Savior, Jesus Christ.

I must tell you during my stay in prison, he kept his promise. He took care of me with the means he had. If it had not been for that, I don't know how I would have survived in there. This man is now my second husband of forty years. There were four years (2014-2018) that we were divorced. We remarried again on August 11, 2019, the same day we first married. My stay was short, but it was long enough for me to learn a lesson I would never forget. I have never gone back to jail or prison since that time.

Breathe: I am praying for you that you realize God always has a ram in the bush. I pray that he is making a way of escape for you right now. I pray when you pass through the waters. He will be with you. That your situations will not overflow you, when you walk through the fires of life, you shall not burn up. For he is the Lord your God that will deliver you out of your Egypt. Isaiah 43:2-3

Seven

I's Married Now

He got out of prison six weeks after I did. We hooked up and dated a year. We got married on August 11, 1976, but I still had not divorced my first husband. I know what you're thinking; I have added bigamist to the list now. My first husband candidly went on with his life and found himself someone else to marry as well. I had two more children for a total of six children, three boys, and three girls. The four I had by my first husband were now split up between his family members. Even though I had married this guy I met in prison, I still had the demons of drugs, alcohol, and sex in my life.

He and I were just two people alike, with familiar spirits operating in us. We liked the very same things. Like I said, we married a year after we met and decided to move on in life. We relocated to Chicago, Illinois calling ourselves starting over. The demons we had, we took them right on to that city with us. We lived in Chicago for twenty years.

October of 1976, we arrived in the city of Chicago. My husband was very familiar with this city because he had an uncle and aunt who lived there. He had spent some time in the Navy in Milwaukee, Wisconsin, near that area. Anyway, we lived with his auntie until we could find jobs. Jobs were hard to find because we lived on the West side of Chicago, and most of the jobs were on Northside. We had to travel a long distance to look for them, and we didn't have transportation. The money we came to Chicago with we used to get back and forth on public transit to job leads.

I will admit that moving to Chicago was one of the biggest challenges in my life. I began to realize it was time to seek a new approach to life. It still took a few more years before it would happen. Although I will give myself credit, I did start working on myself. We both finally found jobs. They weren't much in pay because we didn't have any skills for a lot of the good-paying jobs. Manufacturing work was all we qualified for since our education was limited as well. There was lots of room for improvement within us. God was up to the challenge because He knows the plans He had for both of us; no matter what it looked like, He was still in control.

Eight

Fear or Fear Not

Shortly after we both found jobs, we were asked to leave his auntie's house. So, we searched around in their neighborhood on the Westside of Chicago until we found a rooming house that rented rooms. After securing a room, we moved out, and realization sets in like never before. Fear gripped me like a vice. You may ask why. For the first time in my entire life, I had to grow up. There was no one to lean on, and I didn't know a single soul in that city. It was my man and me, and neither one of us had ever taken responsibility for our lives.

Three years have gone by since we moved, and we secured a decent apartment. We purchased a nice little used car. I became pregnant, which would be my fifth child but my first by him. Reality check! No one around now to leave our child with. We had to step up to the plate and raise this child. My old lifestyle was coming to an end. I pursued getting my GED and a better job as a customer service representative at a large insurance company in the downtown Chicago area.

I finally start realizing I am a wife and a mother. I know what you are thinking, weren't you these things already. The answer would be yes. I was also in my addiction at the time, and I didn't care about being a wife or mother, at least not before I got the reality check in prison. Still, I am fearful because I'm not sure if I can live up to either one because of my past. By this time in my life, I had wasted more than twenty years of my life. I was never sober long enough to know what real life was all about through drugs and alcohol addiction. That thought alone is a sobering one. Don't judge me.

For the very first time in my life, I felt I truly knew what love was. I was in love, and I wanted to learn how to be a wife and a mother to my child that I was carrying. I felt as though I was given a second chance to get things right in life. I had caused so much pain, and it was now time to straighten up my life and allow God to help me on this journey. I was still in the world but doing things differently after being in Chicago for three years.

Breathe: Father, in the name of Jesus, someone is going through life with the feelings of not being good enough. Let them know, Father, that they are worthy. I pray that if you have gone through difficult challenges in your life, you don't give up and continue your journey to the end. Instead, I ask Jesus to strengthen you and give you the courage to change anything in your life that doesn't serve you in the right way.

Nine

Mending the Past

Stay with me now because my eyes are open, and everything in my world is changing. Two more years passed by, and we were blessed in Chicago. In my heart, I wanted to start mending things with my children, whom I had left behind years earlier. I started being convicted in my spirit for not being there for them in life. I began to reach out to the different family members of my first husband, who had my children.

My four children were scattered all over Missouri and parts of Illinois because of the different locations of the various family members. So I started contacting each one and making plans to come and visit my children during the summer when I would have a vacation from my employment.

By this time, my oldest child was thirteen years old. Apparently, the family she lived with was now beginning to experience rebellion and defiance from her. This is a vicious cycle; it was around the same age I became rebellious and defiant. I remember in the summer of 1982, we went back to Missouri to visit our families. While I was in Missouri, I saw my two children that were living with their dad's family members there.

On our return trip home to Chicago, we stopped off in Southern Illinois, where two of my children lived with different families. My eldest child stayed with her dad's aunt, and my youngest son lived with his dad's cousin. I was so glad to see my children on this trip, and we had a pretty decent visit considering our circumstances. The youngest two were still relatively young, so they didn't understand a lot of what was going on.

My oldest daughter expressed her interest in coming back to live with us. As heartbreaking as it was for the family she had been staying with, they agreed to allowed her to live with us. My eldest son came with us too. We found out that he really didn't have anyone who really wanted him to live with them. On our return trip home, I was excited two of the four children I had left behind were now coming to live with me. My heart was rejoicing this must have been the happiest days in my life.

Breathe: I pray for anyone who has faced separation from their children to be reunited in Jesus' name. That you put a hedge of protection around these families and restore their love for one another again. Lord, this is when they need your guidance and strength to get through any tough times they are facing. I pray a blessing to all of those you sent into their lives to help them when they were lost. I pray total restoration upon them in Jesus' name.

Ten

Back in Chicago

Back home in Chicago, my sister-in-law and her three children had come to live with us. I could not wait to get home and rejoice about my kids coming to live with us. Little did I know what was about to take place in my life next would change me forever. My oldest daughter had been living with us for about six months. Shortly after she had come to live with us in our home, my husband started sleeping with her. You see, even though we both had been working, my husband was between jobs. He would take our daughter we had together to preschool and be at home for the older children in the household. His sister and I both worked outside the home.

February 14, 1983, Valentine's Day, a day that I would come to never forget or heal from for a long time. I was at work, and

I decided to call home to wish him a happy Valentine's Day. When he answered the phone, I told him how much I loved him. Suddenly, I paused for a moment because I could hear loud breathing and moans. I asked him who was there, and he denied that anyone was home beside himself. I didn't believe him. I went to my supervisor and told him that I was not feeling well and needed to go home. Yes! You guessed it, molestation had now crept its way into my home right under my nose. I was sleeping with the enemy. He would say he loved me and then turn around and molest my child. I was devastated, hurt and angry all at the same time.

Reflecting back on this horrible thing that had come into my home and remembering that this was the same demon that played a part in my early childhood life. This was a bigger blow than when it happened to me. I was crushed. He was supposed to love me and protect me, and he promised not to do the very thing that he had now done. It crushed me so bad, and I remember when I walked in on him, it took everything inside of me to keep from killing this man.

I want you to know I am having a straight talk with you about my life, what happened to me, and things I had done to others before Christ. At this point, only Christ Jesus could get me through this without me having a murder wrap on my hands. Devastated, crushed, torn to pieces inside, and hurting. I had never felt pain like this before in my life or my heart. What do I do? Where do I go? Who can I turn to? There is nobody here; I am all alone, kept ringing out in my mind. Why me? Why not you? The voice answers back.

Why is this happening to me? Somebody, please, help me; I am about to lose my mind. Help me was the cry that came from way down deep inside of me. I remember the day I confronted this man. I had so much anger and was ready to kill him in the blink of an eye. I had the plot already in my mind on how I was going to kill him. He was not going to get away with doing this to my daughter or me. He needed to pay for what he had done. I couldn't get it out of my mind the murder plot was on. At that moment, I felt someone pulling me out of the room, literally. There was no one but him and me facing death. He or me, it did not matter; I felt life was over anyway.

The next thing I knew, I found myself picking up my keys, heading toward the blue Chevy Nova we owned, getting in, and speeding off as fast as I could down the street. I was crying uncontrollably. I could not believe what had just happened in my life. Crushed! I felt like I could not be put back together again. Why did he do this to me? I continued to drive down the road with all these questions in my mind, compilating suicide and just hurting unbearably. Remembering what it felt like when it happened to me and thinking no one believed me. I caught them, so I know what happened was not a lie. He vowed not to do this and turned on me and did it anyway. The only thing I could see was a death sentence for him. Yes! he didn't deserve to live.

Finally, I was able to pull the car over to the side of the road, and when I looked around me, I was in a park. We had a sunroof top in this car; I remember standing up on the seat through the sunroof and throwing both my hands in the air asking God that day to forgive me of all my sins. Then, with the loudest voice I could, I cried out to Him.

I said, "God if you are real, you have to show me this day. I am going back to that house to kill a man." I wanted to make sure that it reached God's ears in heaven. The very next thing that happens to me was beyond belief. God heard me, and at that moment, He touched me. The only way I can describe it is a liquid love that went all through me. I had never felt anything like that in my life. God had truly touched me until I cried from when I got to that park until late that evening I couldn't stop crying and repenting. Right there in my car Holy Spirit touched me and filled me with His precious Spirit. When I look back at my salvation, it was a plan of God. I traded a jail cell that day for eternal life with Christ Jesus. Hallelujah!

I realized that I needed God in my life, and I was not willing to live or go on another moment without him. Never knew God, didn't even know if He even existed. Heard of Him, never ever talked to Him before now. Only when I was in trouble, I might have said the name Jesus, which really didn't mean that much to me. Never went to church in my early childhood life and was never introduced to him by anyone. Might have gone to church a couple of times because girls I knew in school went to church. It was a way of life for some of them, and they would invite me. But, not me, I didn't want Him; the streets were my god until this happened in my home.

Breathe: God is with you. He will never leave you or forsake you. He will always be there to comfort you throughout life. Many afflictions may come upon your life, but know that He is God, and He will bring you out of them all. I know that things in this life have hurt you to the core of your heart, but you are not forsaken. God is with you. Often, when things don't seem to go right in this life, we start feeling like we've been left on our own. God never promised that our way would always be easy or that His presence with us meant a life of convenience or comfort. But, He did promise over and over in His word that He would be with us in it all and that He would never leave us. He alone holds the power to turn around any difficult season or loss we may be facing and bring great blessing and good through it all.

Eleven

Saved Now

On that day, I received Christ Jesus into my heart and never let him go after that. What I experienced that day was the authentic hand of God on my life. He saved me in a blue Chevy Nova. Hallelujah!! Glory!! My Savior had come when I called on Him. I pulled myself together, and I threw the gun I had away. I went back home, and my husband was waiting for me so that he could discuss with me the pain he had caused. I didn't want to see him. I couldn't even look at him. Even though I wanted to kill him, I did not divorce my husband, nor did I throw away my child again. Finally, he agreed to get counseling, and we would do family counseling.

Christ explained that this newfound love He was showing me I had to extend to them. Please, wait a minute as I write this; I am crying uncontrollably. The Lord is saying to me as I write this book that I am totally set free. I have lived with this for many years, and it still hurt right up until now.

Oh! But! God! He loves me so much; He wants to set me totally free from those demons of pain and hurt that have been in my heart too long. I was able to forgive him, yet the pain has always been there. I never once blamed my daughter for what happened to her. I understood the manipulation of that kind of spirit. I totally blamed him because he was the adult. He was supposed to have loved my children and me in the way a father and husband should.

I wanted my daughter to see a different person within me. Not that same person who walked off and left her in the past. My daughter is now grown. She is fifty years old and has her own family; five beautiful children, four boys, and a girl. My other two children never had the opportunity of returning back to the home after that incident. They were raised entirely by their father's family members. Even though I have my two oldest, they felt I was still not ready to have all my children with me long as this man was there. They looked viewed me a lot worse than what I am expressing in this book. Since I did not kill this man or divorce him, they really thought I was just a fool in love. They did not understand this new me who was saved and filled with the Holy Spirit; they only remembered the bad me. Now that I was showing mercy to my husband and wanting to be there for my daughter, they were saying I must be a fool to put up with this. That I must still be out there doing them drugs.

When God comes into your life, people don't understand who you become in Him. You see, it shows that they are still walking in darkness, and their eyes have not yet been open. The god of this world keeps all of us blinded to the things of the true and living God. I am still being judged to this day by some family members and four of my children. I have told myself for many years to breathe. Take one day at a time and keep on breathing. God is in control, not me. I have tried throughout the years to reach out to them and develop a relationship; it just hasn't worked out yet. I haven't given up on this family; it is in God's timing.

Twelve

Inhale and Exhale

I couldn't divorce him; Jesus was now living inside of me. All the old things were now passing away in my life. I had become a new creature, and God had forgiven me of my sins, and He said in His word that I had to forgive others of their sins against me. Matthew 6:12. The old me would have run away, but, you see, He was revealing who He was to me. My heart would not let me go back into those streets again. He changed my life, and it was changed forever.

I did call the officials; my husband was arrested and taken out of the home. Since I did not have him prosecuted, all of us were referred to family counseling. We went to counseling for over a year. It just seemed to me things were getting worse in the relationship between my daughter and me. The more I tried to reach out to her and show love, the more she rejected me.

No one could understand why I was staying in this toxic relationship. How can this man love you? He has done this, hurting you and your relationship with your children. No one wanted me to continue with my marriage. Some family members blamed me for what happened. I am set free from what people think or feel about it.

My daughter continued to get in trouble. She joined a gang, and arguments escalating more and more in my home. Finally, my sister-in-law found a place and moved out, sending her children back to Missouri to her mother and father. My daughter finally decided that she did not want to live with us anymore and started running away. One thing after another happened in my household.

When looking back, I see that my daughter had a lot of anger inside. I say rightfully so for many reasons. I was still really trying to make up for the past hurt I had caused in our lives and become a mother to her that wasn't there before. Maybe it was too late. I even asked the Lord to help me love my husband once again. I couldn't even judge him. God let me know during my healing time that vengeance was His. (Isaiah 61:2) Right then, I was listening to Holy Spirit about each step I needed to take to keep moving forward.

Breathe: It is not easy to get over hurt and pain. We know patterns are coded into our DNA from previous generations. I break every generational curse that comes upon you and your family. I apply the blood of Jesus to destroy the ancestral DNA in your bloodline. In the name of Jesus, I come against every evil altar erected with your name on it, be destroyed in the blood of Jesus. Every plan of the enemy against your life be destroyed in the blood of Jesus. Every snare, plan, plot, and ploy of the enemy be destroyed in your family bloodline in Jesus' name. No weapon formed against you shall prosper. We claim victory in Jesus' name.

Breathe: The Lord is telling me to let someone know that all things work together for the good of those who love Him. God is working everything out for you and your family right now. The Lord is able to mend broken hearts and heal you of all your hurt and pain. It will not be easy. I just encourage you, no matter what, to continue moving forward. It will get easier as time goes on.

Thirteen

Voice of God

The Lord let me know what had happened; He allowed it to happen, and I shouldn't give up on my family. I could not believe what I was hearing from the Lord. I burst out in prayer and asked God, what do you mean you allowed this to happen. He said, "let's have some straight talk now that I have your attention." I started sobbing uncontrollably; my Father laid it on me. Before I was ever conceived in my mother's womb, He let me know that He had purposed for these things to happen in my life. It was the only thing that would crush me enough for Him to get what He wanted out of my life. That was total obedience to Him for His name's sake. Still, I did not understand this God I had just come to know, who knew the plans He already destined for my life. With Him being God, He could have spared me from many things that happened to me in my life.

God was the potter, and I was the clay. He was molding and shaping my life for His glory. God had a different plan for my life, and it was to bring Him glory in the hard times and even the bad times. He wanted me to learn how to trust Him and to lean on Him. God knows the plans He has for each of us. No matter what it looks like, He is still God and is in control. He wanted to reveal His wisdom to me and give me understanding. He revealed to me real love that I had never had in life. That agape love, unconditional, and you can't receive it from anyone else. Remember, I was in search of love ever since when I was a little girl. The things that happened to me started me looking for love in all the wrong places. I thought it was in the world. No, it was right there with me all the time. All I had to do was reach inside and let it cometh forth.

Breathe: God is about to change someone's life forever. You have been going through for years and still waiting to see the hand of God in your life. God says, "I am breathing on you right now. The miracle you've been seeking is upon you right now. All you have to do is believe and not doubt. I am your God who cannot fail; this is your coming out season. Nothing can hurt you or hold you back from the plans I set in order for you." (Jeremiah 29:11)

Fourteen

Eyes on Jesus

I was in search of me a church to join. I needed another kind of family. So, I started attending church regularly. I continued counseling even though my daughter and husband did not want to go. I knew that I had the Lord now, and I still wanted to continue my healing process. The Lord had my attention; now, I had to learn how to read His Word to know when He was speaking into my life. I needed desperately to keep my relationship going with Him.

Hooked on Jesus; I couldn't live without Him now. Some may call me a Jesus freak, but that's alright with me too. It no longer mattered what people said anymore; it only mattered what Jesus had to say. I had lived a life full of darkness, and now the light had come in. I was ready to let his light shine in me. He was now my Savior, my husband, and my friend. The world was behind me; I had hurt enough people. I had done enough evil to last me a lifetime. And now I was taking a stand and saying no more to the devil's work.

Breathe: Somebody out there has come to the end of the road, in the midst of making a decision. I don't know what you are going through or have been through. But, I can be a witness that Jesus is the way, the truth, and the life. Let Him come and live in you. Open your heart and let Him in. He will guide and lead you into all truth. He will never forsake you or leave you alone. I say to you while you are standing in that place, try Jesus. He has never failed anyone.

Fifteen

Life in Christ

Now that I am living in Christ Jesus and Christ Jesus is living in me, it changes everything in my life. Everything I ever thought I was looking for was in Him. Love, Hope, Peace, Joy, Prosperity, Deliverance, and Salvation. The love I was looking for now living inside of me. It is the love that I chose to show others, no matter if they have done anything to me are not.

I believe that you may represent the closest thing to Christ Jesus some people will ever see. I am a living example before my family that Jesus is real, and He can change you if you allow Him to. I can see the hand of God in everything that ever happened to me.

In this book, I shared what led to my salvation, that which

Holy Spirit wanted me to share. I hope those who are a part of my life can see beyond the bad things that happened and see the good. So that they too can come to some closure regarding the way life was dealt them. Since my salvation took place, I've come to learn that we owe no man anything but LOVE.

These weren't the only things that happened to me while living in darkness. But, it served as the very thing that broke me and crushed me for Jesus to get the glory out of my life. For me, it was the straw that broke the curses that were operating in my life. Only darkness can happen when you are living without Christ Jesus, the Light. It has been over 35 years since I have given my life to Christ Jesus, and I haven't looked back into the world, not one time.

Let me tell you when the Lord saves you, you are saved once and for all. The things I use to do I don't do anymore. I have forgiven everyone that ever hurt me, and I pray someday they will forgive me for what I have done to them. I learned once I got in Christ that unforgiveness is bondage for you and the other person. Forgiveness is for you, not the other person, because it brings you total freedom from that thing.

> **Breathe**: Lord, I ask that you continue to help the one who needs to forgive and the one that needs forgiveness. We all fall short of the glory of God. I am asking that You show Your unconditional love in the person's heart.

And forgive us our debts, as we also have forgiven our debtors. And lead us not into temptation but deliver us from the evil one. For if you forgive other people when they sin against you, your Heavenly Father will also forgive you. But if you do not forgive others their sins, your Father will not forgive your sins. **Matthew 6:12-15**

I have become transparent and willing to share my story. It doesn't have to be your story, but I am sure someone will be able to breathe a little easier after engaging in my story.

Sixteen

The Power of Real Love

The power of real love is the love that comes only from Jesus. He proved His love when He willingly went to the cross and died for the whole world. His love is unconditional, and there are no hidden motives. He took on all the pain, suffering, and sin for us all. Even when we face trials and tribulations in our own lives, He is the answer to whatever it is or was. The power of real love sees no faults; it sees beyond our faults and sees our needs. He knows the condition of every human being. He saw me in that brokenness, and when I called on Him, He demonstrated the power of real love to me. What the devil meant for harm in my life, God turned it around for His glory. I didn't know or see God's plans, but He knew what plans He had for me. He also knows the plans He has for my husband and children.

Beloved, let us love one another, for love is from God, and whoever loves has been born of God and knows God. Anyone who does not love does not know God, because God is love. **1 John 4:7-8**

God's very essence is love. When we love one another, we are fulfilling God's most fundamental wish for our lives.

I am only testifying about His goodness in my life. He has turned my life around, not allowing me to die out there in my sins. I am so grateful to the Lord for His goodness to me. This one thing I do know, in the words of King David.

"Taste and see that the Lord is good, blessed is the man that trust in him." **Psalm 34:8**

Breathe: Heavenly Father, I pray that you bless the one reading this book right now. He that has an ear to hear let them hear what the Spirit of the living God is saying through me right now. Let go of your life of darkness and give your life to Christ Jesus. He will look after you in every situation that you may be going through. In every dark cloud, there is also light. Jesus is waiting for you to make a choice this day whom you will serve. I pray that it will be Him because He loves you. May the peace of God rest, rule, and abide in your lives. Amen!

Seventeen

Affirmation

I pray that it fills you with love, hope, and faith as I end my life story. I am asking you to complete this brief meditation with an affirmation for your life. I want you to sit in a room free of distractions with your body comfortably seated. I want you to close your eyes and begin to gently breathe in and out through your nostrils. Bring your awareness to your heart. As you do this, allow the breathing to continue in and out of your nostrils.

Focus your attention on this area as the breath has its own rhythm in out of your body. I want you to begin visualizing the petals of your heart chakra gently opening. Now see your heart filling with light. You're allowing love to fill your heart, pushing out any past hurts with each breathe. If you have any pain or disease of the body, visualize the love traveling to that area. Visualize healing for this part of your body. Visualize this love from your heart, expanding throughout every aspect of your being. Continue breathing as you fill your heart with light and love. I want you to repeat this affirmation to yourself three times: my body, mind, and spirit are healing now. The next affirmation I want you to repeat three times is: the power of Love is healing me on all levels of my being. Breathe in and out. Let these words fill your body with light. Letting it heal all aspects of your being with light and love.

Take ten full deep breathes into this energy, breathing in, breathing out, at your own pace. Now begin to return back to the body, gently bringing awareness back to the room. Feel gratitude for this healing for yourself and for being here right now. Open Your Eyes. I want you to know everything will get better. Breathe, keep giving yourself permission to breathe, Shalom!

Prayer Declarations

My prayer for you is that God breathes in your spirit the fresh wind of His anointing. Breathe healing for your families and for our land. Father continue to breathe the breath of life into our spirits. Breathe Holy Spirit, let the wind of your breath living inside of us become a tsunami of Your glory! I recognize You doing something new inside of me. I receive all that you are doing in me, and I look forward to growing and knowing you better. Knowing who you really are.

I love, trust, and praise You, Lord. You are my Strength, my Rock, and my Deliverer. When I call upon You in my time of trouble, You will hear and answer me. I know that You will never fail nor forsake me. Teach me your ways. I'm still breathing....

Prayer of Paul

For this cause I bow my knees unto the Father of our Lord Jesus Christ, Of whom the whole family in heaven and earth is named, That he would grant you, according to the riches of his glory, to be strengthened with might by his Spirit in the inner man; That Christ may dwell in your hearts by faith; that ye, being rooted and grounded in love, May be able to comprehend with all saints what is the breadth, and length, and depth and height; And to know the love of Christ, which passes knowledge, that ye might be filled with all the fullness of God. Now unto him that is able to do exceeding, abundantly above all that we ask or think, according to the power that worketh in us. Unto him be glory in the church by Christ Jesus throughout all ages, world with end. Amen.
Ephesians 3:14-21

Meet Apostle Pearlie Walker

Apostle Pearlie Walker received a Certificate of Pastoral Ordination from Christian Body Life Fellowship. She has also received a Certificate of Apostle Ordination from New Beginnings Church of God Apostolic Faith, Inc. She attended Epic Bible College in Sacramento, California where she studied the basic history of the old and new testament of the bible.

Apostle Pearlie set aside her ministry until she and her family could settle in Vacaville, California.

On August 8, 1993, Apostle Pearlie Walker and her family moved from Bloomington/Normal Illinois to Vacaville, California. Through the Grace of God's hand, the family has walked through a brief stay at the Opportunity House, a homeless shelter. She joined a small church called "Flames of Fire", where she was a member for a short time.

In 1997, she was ordained as a Pastor under the Leadership of Bishop Jackie Austin at the Holy Deliverance Powerhouse Establishment Ministries in Sacramento, California. Apostle Pearlie Walker encounter a setback when her Certificate of Ordination record was destroyed. Soon after obtained a new Certificate of Ordination was given by Christian Body Life Fellowship. Bishop Jackie Austin at the Holy Deliverance Powerhouse Establishment

Ministries released Apostle Pearlie Walker to start her own church.

In 1998, Apostle Pearlie Walker started her ministry called "Now is the Time Ministries". With all authority in heaven and earth, she taught a bible study group and became a part of Vacaville Christian Life Center Prison Ministry under the Leadership of Pastor Tim Mays. Apostle Pearlie Walker began her own show on Vacaville's cable access, called "Pearlie Walker Ministries".

On February 24, 2000, she became the Senior Pastor of "In His Word Church" located in Dixon, California. Apostle Pearlie Walker's ministry reaches across Northern California. She also teaches in the following ministry areas:
Prayer Conferences
Healing and deliverance conferences
Preaching
Teaching the Word of God
Spiritual counseling
Women Ministry

Apostle Pearlie Walker Ministries is in transition being led by the Holy Spirit. The ministry is mobile.

https://inhiswordchurch623.wixsite.com/inhiswordchurch/about-pearlie-walker-ministries

www.ingramcontent.com/pod-product-compliance
Lightning Source LLC
Chambersburg PA
CBHW071838290426
44109CB00017B/1860